NFL RIVALRIES

PATRIOTS VS. JETS

By Paul Bowker

Kaleidoscope
Minneapolis, MN

Your Front Row Seat to the Games

This edition first published in 2020 by Kaleidoscope Publishing, Inc.

For information regarding permission, write to
Kaleidoscope Publishing, Inc.
6012 Blue Circle Drive
Minnetonka, MN 55343

Library of Congress Control Number
2019939219

ISBN
978-1-64519-083-7 (library bound)
978-1-64494-168-3 (paperback)
978-1-64519-184-1 (ebook)

Printed in the United States of America.

TABLE OF CONTENTS

CHAPTER 1

A Stunning Twist

Bill Belichick stepped to a **podium**. It was January 4, 2000. Belichick was speaking to reporters. He was the new head coach of the New York Jets. But what he had to say surprised everyone.

National Football League (NFL) coaching jobs are hard to get. Belichick had been a Jets assistant. The team long planned to **promote** him. Finally, it was his time. But he had doubts. The team ownership was changing. Belichick talked with his family that morning. He told them he was turning the job down.

But he had not yet told the Jets.

Bill Belichick, left, was hired as a New York Jets assistant coach in 1997.

Just a few months after the press conference, Belichick was on the sidelines coaching for the rival Patriots.

Belichick was nervous. He wrote a note on a napkin. He handed the napkin to a team official. It said he was quitting. And then he stepped to the podium.

Reporters watched closely. Cameras flashed. Then Belichick spoke.

"I'm resigning from the New York Jets," he said.

The team was stunned. So were fans. But what came next made them feel even worse. On January 27, the New England Patriots hired a new coach. It was Belichick. One of the NFL's strongest rivalries just got stronger.

Belichick had a lot of work to do. The Patriots were not a great team. He led his team to New York in Week 2. The Jets won by a single point. The Jets then beat the Patriots again in Week 7. New York finished the season with nine wins. New England had just five.

Things quickly changed. The 2001 Patriots went on a run. Belichick led them all the way to the **Super Bowl**. New England won. And the Patriots were far from done. They won five more in the next 18 years. That tied the record for the most ever. And the Jets did not even make it to the big game once.

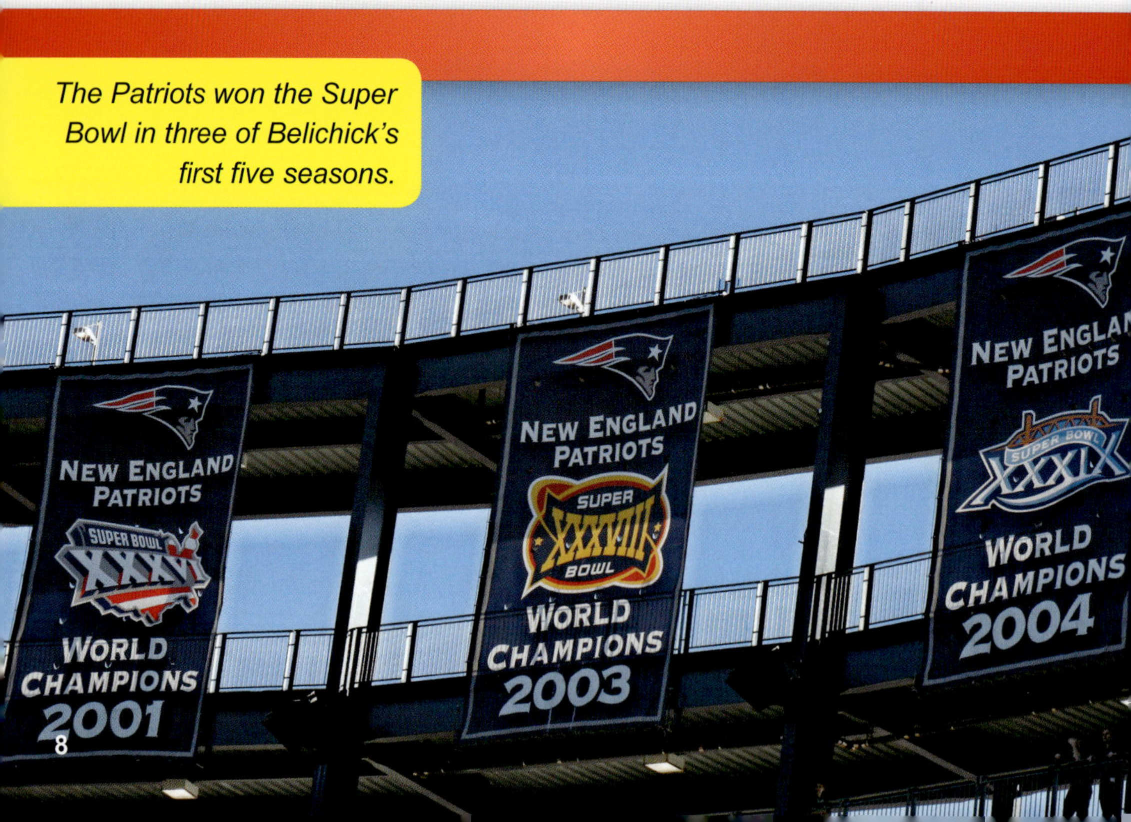

The Patriots won the Super Bowl in three of Belichick's first five seasons.

HEAD TO HEAD

STATS

Through the 2018 season

JETS		PATRIOTS
53	WINS	63
45.7	WINNING PERCENTAGE	54.3
2409	POINTS SCORED	2694
1	PLAYOFF WINS	2
9 (1966–70)	LONGEST WIN STREAK	(2003–06) 7
1	TOTAL SUPER BOWL VICTORIES	6

CHAPTER 2

The Jets wore throwback uniforms from 2007–09 and in 2011 in their original Titans colors.

Hot Start

The Jets began life as the New York Titans. The Patriots were the Boston Patriots. They first met September 17, 1960. The Titans were just seconds away from a win. They were at home at the Polo Grounds in New York City. They led the Patriots 24–21. Only twelve seconds remained. But the Titans faced fourth down. They had to **punt**.

If they won, they would be 2–0. But disaster struck. The center **snapped** the ball. Titans punter Rick Sapienza fumbled it. He was never able to get a kick off.

Patriots defender Chuck Shonta recovered the ball. Then he started running. He ran 52 yards into the end zone. Touchdown! Gino Cappelletti added an extra point. That gave the Patriots a 28–24 win.

It was the Patriots' first win over New York. It was a fitting start to the rivalry. The game came down to its final play. And the Titans did not like it. They thought the play should have been stopped. They said a Patriots player kicked the ball. That was against the rules. It should have stopped play. The rivalry would only heat up from there.

FUN FACT
The Titans shared the Polo Grounds with the New York Mets baseball team.

Patriots receiver and kicker Gino Cappelletti was the American Football League Most Valuable Player in 1964.

Both teams had started in a new league. The American Football League (AFL) began in 1960. It had eight teams. The Patriots and Titans quickly became rivals. That was no surprise. The cities already had a strong rivalry in baseball. The Boston Red Sox and New York Yankees had been playing for years.

The Titans became the Jets in 1963. Five years later, they won the Super Bowl. They were the first AFL team to win it. Three years later, the Boston Patriots became the New England Patriots. A lot changed in those first few years. But the Jets-Patriots rivalry never did.

New England also wore throwbacks from the Boston Patriots days from 2009 to 2012.

Rivalry Map

N
W
E
S
New Hampshire
Maine
Vermont
New England Patriots
Gillette Stadium
Foxborough,
Massachusetts
New York Jets
MetLife Stadium
East Rutherford,
New Jersey
Rhode Island
Connecticut
Pennsylvania
New Jersey
Ohio
Delaware
Maryland
West
Virginia
Virginia
North Carolina
South Carolina

CHAPTER 3

Brady Leads the Way

Drew Bledsoe was in trouble. No receivers were open. The Patriots quarterback scrambled. He headed toward the sidelines. Little stood out about the play. It came in the team's second game of the 2001 season. But it changed football forever.

Bledsoe headed out of bounds. Jets **linebacker** Mo Lewis was in position. He slammed into the quarterback. Bledsoe tried to keep playing. But he was too hurt to continue. Bledsoe was bleeding internally. He almost died.

The Patriots had no choice. They turned to their unknown backup. Tom Brady jogged onto the field. He could not lead a comeback. New York won 10–3. Yet Jets fans might have wished that day had never happened.

Drew Bledsoe became the Patriots' all-time passing leader on October 1, 2000.

Tom Brady tries to avoid two Jets defenders in a 2002 game.

Brady started again one week later. This time New England won. Brady never lost his starting job. He went on to become the most successful quarterback ever. In February 2019, the Patriots faced the Los Angeles Rams. Behind Brady, they won. It marked Brady's sixth Super Bowl victory. No other quarterback had even won five.

Brady saved some of his best moments for the Jets. He lost in that first game. Then he won twenty-seven of his next thirty-three games against New York.

THE SUPER BOWL MOMENT

The Jets have won a single title. They won Super Bowl III after the 1968 season. Star quarterback "Broadway Joe" Namath led the way. Fifty years later, the NFL celebrated that win. The tribute came at Super Bowl 53. The Patriots won the game. The worst part for Jets fans was at the end. Namath had to hand the Super Bowl trophy to the Patriots.

Before Brady, the Patriots often struggled. From 1966 to 1973, they lost seventeen of nineteen games against the Jets. That made for a one-sided rivalry. Things really heated up in the 2000s. Both teams had successful seasons. And the Jets had a hot young quarterback, too.

Mark Sanchez took over in 2009. The Jets won two of their next four games against New England. The fifth was the biggest. Both teams made the playoffs after the 2010 season. They met in the second round. The Jets talked trash leading up to the game. Then Sanchez backed it up. He passed for three touchdowns. The Jets won, 28–21.

Mark Sanchez went 2–6 against the Pats in the regular season but beat them in a playoff game in January 2011.

CHAPTER 4

Bad Blood

The 2007 season opener was coming up. The Patriots were coming to town. And Jets coach Eric Mangini was nervous. The Patriots were one of the best teams in the league. But Mangini had other concerns. Coaches signal plays in the NFL. He thought the Patriots might be recording the Jets coaches. This is illegal in the NFL. So Mangini told the security team at Giants Stadium.

Giants Stadium was the site of one of the most famous moments in Jets-Patriots history.

FUN FACT
Mangini was familiar with the Patriots tactics because he had been an assistant coach there under Bill Belichick.

Security officials found the Patriots recording on the sidelines. They took the camera. NFL officials would review the tape later. The Patriots won 38–14. But the real story was happening off the field. The players were done battling. But employees from both teams were screaming at each other. The tape showed the Patriots breaking the rules.

The Patriots were in trouble. They lost a first-round draft pick. The NFL fined Belichick $500,000. The NFL fined the Patriots $250,000. Belichick never spoke to Mangini after that. The event is known today as "Spygate."

The rivalry has been fueled in many ways. Coaches changed sides. Players changed sides. Fans yelled at each other. In some ways, the rivalry is natural. The teams play just 200 miles (322 km) apart. New Yorkers and New Englanders are rivals in a lot of ways. But the best part of the rivalry comes on the field.

The Patriots-Jets rivalry is fueled by passionate fans on both sides.

Jets-Patriots games have featured some crazy finishes. They nearly played to a tie in a 2015 game. It went into overtime. The Patriots won the coin toss. They could have taken the ball. They instead chose to kick. The Jets got the ball. They scored. They won the game.

There will be more surprising finishes to come. That much is certain in this rivalry.

In 2018, for the third year in a row, the Patriots won both meetings with the Jets.

THE BUTT FUMBLE

It's Thanksgiving Day in 2012. A Jets play breaks down. Quarterback Mark Sanchez tries to run. He runs into the back side of offensive lineman Brandon Moore. Sanchez loses the ball in the collision. Steve Gregory of the Patriots picks the ball up. He returns it 32 yards for a touchdown. The play is nicknamed the "Butt Fumble." The score was one of three touchdowns scored in 52 seconds by New England. The Patriots won, 49–19.

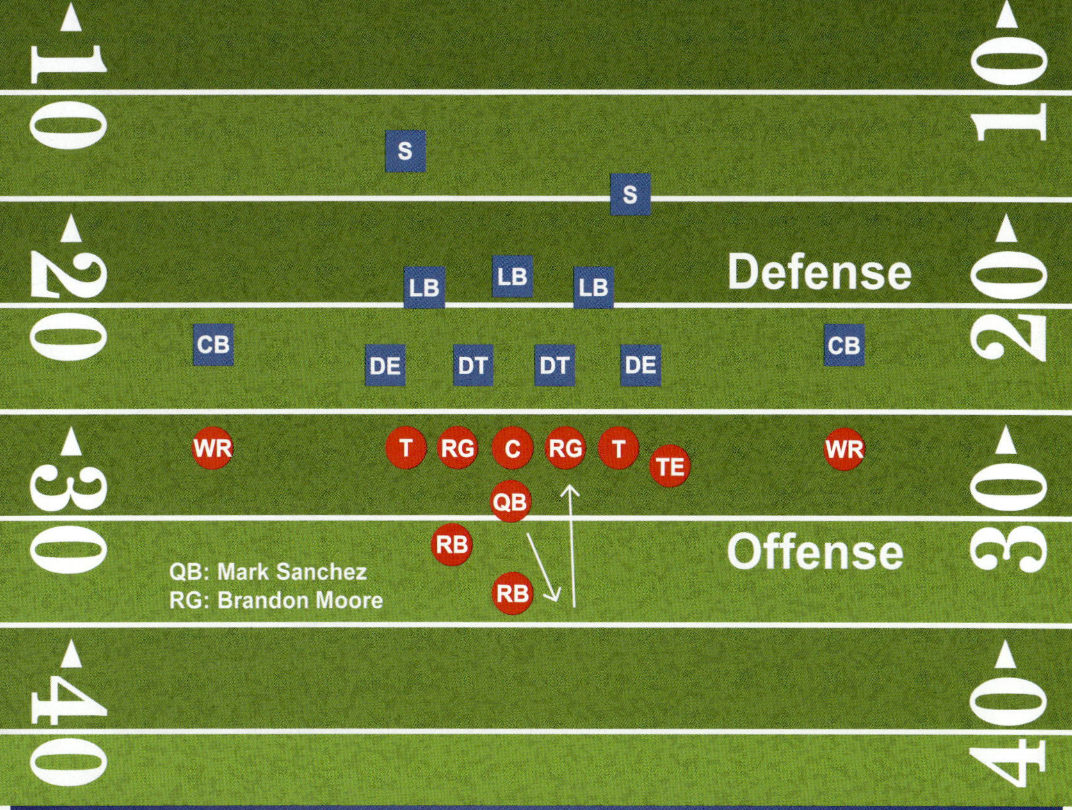

BEYOND THE BOOK

After reading the book, it's time to think about what you learned. Try the following exercises to jumpstart your ideas.

THINK

THAT'S NEWS TO ME. Chapter One talks about Bill Belichick's decision to quit the New York Jets after just one day as head coach. How might news sources be able to fill in more detail about this? What new information could you find in news articles? Where could you go to find those sources?

CREATE

SHARPEN YOUR RESEARCH SKILLS. The first Patriots vs. Jets game was played in 1960. Where could you go in the library to find more information about the rivalry? Who could you talk to who might know more? Create a research plan. Write a paragraph about your next steps.

SHARE

SUM IT UP. Write one paragraph summarizing the important points from this book. Make sure it's in your own words. Don't just copy what is in the text. Share the paragraph with a classmate. Does your classmate have any comments about the summary? Do they have additional questions about the Patriots-Jets rivalry?

GROW

REAL-LIFE RESEARCH. What places could you visit to learn more about the Patriots-Jets rivalry? What other things could you learn while you were there?

Visit www.ninjaresearcher.com/0837 to learn how to take your research skills and book report writing to the next level!

RESEARCH

SEARCH LIKE A PRO
Learn about how to use search engines to find useful websites.

FACT OR FAKE?
Discover how you can tell a trusted website from an untrustworthy resource.

TEXT DETECTIVE
Explore how to zero in on the information you need most.

SHOW YOUR WORK
Research responsibly—learn how to cite sources.

WRITE

GET TO THE POINT
Learn how to express your main ideas.

PLAN OF ATTACK
Learn prewriting exercises and create an outline.

DOWNLOADABLE REPORT FORMS

Further Resources

BOOKS

Blumberg, Saulie. *New York Jets*. Abdo Publishing, 2017.

Whiting, Jim. *New England Patriots*. Abdo Publishing, 2017.

Wilner, Barry. *NFL's Top Ten Rivalries*. Abdo Publishing, 2017.

WEBSITES

Factsurfer.com gives you a safe, fun way to find more information.

1. Go to www.factsurfer.com.
2. Enter "Patriots vs. Jets" into the search box and click 🔍.
3. Select your book cover to see a list of related websites.

Glossary

contract: A contract is an agreement between a team and player or coach about how much that employee will be paid. Bill Belichick had a contract with the Jets to become head coach.

linebacker: A linebacker is a player who defends passes and runs by the other team. The linebacker hit Drew Bledsoe and knocked him out of the game.

podium: A podium is a platform positioned at the front of a room so that the speaker is in front of and higher than seated people in the room. Bill Belichick stepped up to the podium.

promote: When a team chooses to promote someone, they give that person a better job. The Jets wanted to promote Bill Belichick in 2000.

punt: A punt happens when a player kicks the ball to the other team. The Patriots were stopped on third down and chose to punt.

snapped: The ball is snapped to start a play when the center hands or pitches the ball backward to another player. David Andrews snapped the ball to Tom Brady.

Super Bowl: The Super Bowl is a championship game played each year between the two best teams in the National Football League. The Jets have won one Super Bowl in their history.

Index

PHOTO CREDITS

The images in this book are reproduced through the courtesy of: Julio Cortez/AP Images, front cover (left); Ric Tapia/AP Images, front cover (right); EFKS/Shutterstock Images, front cover (background); wacpan/Shutterstock, p. 3; Adam Nadel/AP Images, pp. 4–5; Al Messerschmidt/AP Images, pp. 6–7; charnsitr/Shutterstock, p. 7; Steve Broer/Shutterstock, p. 8; Red Line Editorial, pp. 9, 15, 27; Paul Spinelli/AP Images, p. 10; Jeff Bukowski/Shutterstock, p. 11; catwalker/Shutterstock, p. 12; NFL Photos/AP Images, p. 13; Elise Amendola/AP Images, pp. 14, 20–21; MG SG/Shutterstock, p. 16; Kevin Higley/AP Images, p. 17; Kathy Willens/AP Images, p. 18; Joseph Sohm/Shutterstock, pp. 22–23, 25; Michael Dwyer/AP Images, pp. 24–25; Damian Strohmeyer/AP Images, p. 26; dean bertoncelj/Shutterstock, p. 30.

ABOUT THE AUTHOR

Paul Bowker is a sports editor and children's book author who was raised in Massachusetts and is now living in Mississippi. He has covered hundreds of NFL games, including many games between the Patriots and Jets.